Mother

Poems from Motherhood

Mother
Poems from Motherhood

for my son, Canyon

Linda Keller

"My Son" first appeared in *New Beginnings* (La Leche League), 1992.

© 2015 Linda Keller

Graphic design by John Boak

Library of Congress Control Number: 2015904227

ISBN 978-0-9625718-7-9

ALSO BY LINDA KELLER

Take It & Go On
Comet Dreams
Deep in the Wilderness
You Can Stop Longing

CHAPBOOKS
Here I Am
Making Up the Way

Table of Contents

Fertile Dreams   1

Invitation   2

The Hallway Between the Doors   5

Canyon   7

A New Morse Code   8

A New Light   10

My Son   12

My Arms Won't Let Go   15

Nine Months Old   16

First Tooth   19

Poem to an Expectant Mother   21

Almost a Year Old   22

Time to Wean   24

Two Years Old   26

Two and a Half Years Old   28

Making Valentines with My Five Year Old Son   30

Your Daughter   32

Lost   35

Haiku   37

The Last Piano Recital   38

One Thing   40

Quiet Future   42

The Stars on the Ceiling   45

Epilogue   47

Author   49

Dedication   51

Recommendations   52

Fertile Dreams

I dream now of green
in its many shades:
the bright green of banana tree leaves,
the pale green of succulent vines
creeping along the beach,
the dark green of lantana bushes,
splashed with delicate orange and pink flowers,
the green of ohia trees delighting bees
with their fuzzy red blossoms,
the flying green of petite anianiau birds.
These greens show the fertile earth below,
how much we can grow in ideal soil.
These greens tell me of my own fertility,
entice me to plant seeds,
to risk living in bright color.

The Invitation

To John

Faith approached fear and said,
"Let me show you the steps
to this dance."
Fear accepted with hesitation,
but allowed herself to relax
into the guiding arms of faith.

As they danced,
fears were surpassed by visions:
visions of big eyes filled with wonder at the
sight of ducks and squirrels,
visions of a child
being lifted into the air, smiling,
visions of singing songs
that rhyme and reading stories.
Fears tried to re-surface,
thinking of feet growing into new shoes,
of pediatrician visits and measles,
of the end to quiet, tea-sipping breakfasts,
of inevitable adolescence.
Faith held her closer and said,
"you can face each challenge."

My love, faith has won.
Take me in your arms,
lead me in the dance
we've never done,
the one that brings our love
to a visible swelling,
and then,
a new voice.

The Hallway Between the Doors

Caught in a nine month hallway
I see a new door in the distance.

Though I walk with expectations
like those of a child
the day before Christmas,
I feel a twinge of sadness
as the door of my girlhood
swings shut,
the memory of
an extended adventure
receding.

Canyon

Canyon
a name I imagine
for a boy child
solid rock
shaped by rivers flow

Canyon
a place I climb
feet crunching across chips of
smooth sandstone
fingers looking for holes to grip

Canyon
a wide channel
with sandy bottom
paths leading above
to ancient homes,
a place to rest and store thoughts

Canyon
cut by the river of my feelings
flowing steadily forward, forward,
to a deep pool,
a place where I can begin again

A New Morse Code

A thin brown line runs
from my newly pushed out
belly button up to my chest,
a record of your presence.
I lie back in the tub,
watching as, on the right side,
my belly protrudes,
then on the left, the quick blip of a rising foot.
I splash the warm water over me,
pat where your foot just kicked.
It kicks again.
I giggle.
We communicate like this —
a different sort of Morse code:
kicks, pats and giggles —
a pattern which guarantees
I put my cares aside
simply to enjoy your presence inside me.
It is temporary.
Days have passed into eight months already.
Soon you will be on the outside,
cord cut,
breathing on your own.

I wonder sometimes if you can feel
what I feel,
this love for the fruit of my belly,
for this new Morse code.

A New Light

The tracks left in the grass
from the gardener's truck
look like faded yellow ribbons.
The frost damaged flowers
have been removed,
leaving only the clumps of dirt
turned for next spring's planting.
The squirrel without a tail
leaps out onto the path,
hoping for peanuts,
but my hands are as empty
as the flower beds.
I look to the top of the tree
he climbs,
with its colors of zucchini and corn.
I hear the definitive sound of autumn
as my feet pass through dry leaves
on this day of my birth
thirty-seven years ago.

I move through them,
toward the birth of my son,
due to arrive in five weeks,
noting the season's change
in a new light.

My Son

Your head fits in the curve under my chin,
I nuzzle against the soft fuzz of your hair,
noticing the little things about you —
the way your hand grasps tight the collar of my shirt,
the huff huff of your short breaths,
the way your eyes open so wide I can see the whites
above the pupil as you stare at a stuffed raccoon,
the way your forehead wrinkles as you
try to look up at my face,
the way your hands roam
like wild animals without direction.
I notice these little things about you —
the way your feet kick at my arm and your head
turns frantically from side to side as you search
for the source of nourishment,
the glub glub sound of you swallowing my milk,
one hand clasping the center of my bra,
the way your eyelids slowly lower as you
suck the manna from my breast,
the way you later sleep on my chest,
a warm ball in my arms.

I think of how soon this will pass,
you will grow too big for this space.
I notice these things and think of all the years
I feared to have you in my life,
you, an angel with petal velvet skin,
you, with brightest eyes focused on mine,
you, with mouth making "o" shapes
and the sounds of your tiny squeaks and grunts,
you, who have made my love rise,
a full river flooding the bank of my heart,
my son, my precious son.

My Arms Won't Let Go

You've fallen asleep in my arms.
I'm reading, gently rocking you.
Then I lift you for a burp.
You settle into my shoulder, a living
chair for your leaning head.
More connected than separate,
we rock to the rhythm of our breath.
Finally, I stand up, walk to your room.
But my arms won't let go.
I stand there a few more minutes,
gently swaying,
listening to you breathe.
My cheek presses against yours,
as I breathe in this brief time
where you are happy in my arms.
All the tasks I could be doing
line up like unassembled parts
on a conveyor belt.
I turn it off, choosing instead to walk
quietly through the house,
holding you close.
Then, slowly, I return to your room,
lift you over the crib railing
and tuck the blankets around you.

Nine Months Old

You push up on your hands
and lurch forward,
eager as a puppy in the park,
belly flopping your way
across the floor
where I lie with your book.
It's a favorite of yours
with all its brightly colored
opening parts: a door with
a bear behind it, a lion
under the stairs, a spotted
snake in the closet.
I say, "Is he behind the door?
NOOOOOO!"
We turn the pages,
discovering exotic animals
in their unlikely places,
but not Spot,
arriving finally at the box
whose lid is half torn off.
This was the one you learned to open first.
Now all the openable parts boast tape repairs.

But it is the look on your face
as you scoot across the room
imprinted on my own mind's page.

A week later, you've learned to stand.

First Tooth

The basin across from me
was shaped like a big pair
of lips: two symmetrical pointy
peaks formed the cupie bow top.
The tree line ended in a perfect
curve along the bottom
like the line of the lower lip.
I lay back in the tundra waiting,
as if the earth might blow me a kiss,
watching the shadows create
body parts out of mountains:
legs bent up at the knees, the curve of a hip,
the jagged ridge behind the lips
my baby's first tooth.

Poem to an Expectant Mother

Joy blooms inside you,
prepares for its passage,
a push into the world.

Joy will bloom outside you,
in the music of a tiny laugh,
in the scent of sweet milk breath,
in a poem daily written
by the changing new life in your world.

Almost a Year Old

I remember when we were two people
in one body, belted waists
expanding into elastic as you grew.
I remember feeling like a bowling
ball was stuck in the birth canal
as I pushed you toward your first breath.
You looked first at me, then your dad,
linking faces to voices
you'd heard from the womb.
I remember your face in the middle of the
night as the nurse brought you to my bed,
your eyes brightly awake, your head
craning for my breast.
I remember carrying you out of the hospital
into your first whiff of cool November air.
I remember the digital clock next to the bed
as I woke for your feedings:
2:00 a.m., 4:00 a.m., 6:00 a.m.,
the warmth of your tiny body
lying next to mine, how I'd fold back the
sheet to keep it from covering your head.

I remember afternoon naps, the days
before you could roll or crawl,
when you could sleep chest-to-chest
in my arms without your head hanging
over my shoulder.

These are the seeds I store.
Even when you have grown bigger
than your dad, I will remember.
I will remember when we were two people
in one body,
the time when we were linked
mouth to breast,
what you taught me about connection.

Time to Wean

The tyranny
of nipple to mouth
a once cherished flow,
now souring with
the demand of two-year-old
insistance.

I'm sore.
Exhausted.
My arm has fallen asleep,
your hair sweaty from
leaning against it.

Even in your sleep,
you cry out, "No!"
when I try to put you down.

For twenty-one months
these drops of milk
have flowed willingly
into your mouth,
the time when they would
end seeming so far into the
future.

Excitement mixes
with knowing tears—
we are at the end of
nursing.

Two Years Old

Taw-daw.
Shan-do-done.
Pa-po-mint.

Words
peek out of your mouth,
syllables of your own
invention.

A little high voice
reserved for inanimate
objects brings bunnies, trains
and trolls into the world
of conversation.

More of dat.
Wee-oo.
Ba-ee.

Vowels whirl
like the blender
that fascinates you.

Bumby.
Yo-urt.
Bobble.

I listen
knowing that someday
you will speak
a more common language.
Your charming pronunciations
will be a part of some distant past,
a past when daily
you would lift
your arms up,
when I would hear
"mamoo, mamoo, mamoo"
with frequency and volume,
when I was the center of
your world,
and you were becoming
less and less the center
of mine.

Two and a Half Years Old

The little holes at the bottom
of each side of the slide
make the perfect spot
for you to plug in your
tree bridges.
You climb up the
chain ladder,
pause at the top
of the platform
wearing a big grin,
then with one whoosh,
we hear the snap
of branches breaking
and your laugh of glee!

Like a proud inventor,
you show the bridge/slide
game to another boy
at the playground.
His face wears the same smile
as he whooshes and snaps
his way down the slide.

What magic you bring
to the ordinary,
no fancy apparatus
required,
just a hole,
a branch,
and the desire to play!

Whoosh, snap, whoosh, snap!
We set the bridges
in place again and again,
as you show me
how simple it is
to have fun.

Making Valentines
with My Five Year Old Son

Dots of cinnamon, cherry
and lemon from your
"smelly" markers decorate
the borders of your
orange hearts.

You stop,
mindful as a detective,
think of who it is for,
then draw in the centers.
For your teacher,
a petroglyph boy
climbs the slide.
For your best friend,
a swing soars high
as a pop-up fly.
For grandma,
it's your trademark
elevator, complete
with criss cross gates.

Spelling aloud
you write each letter
of your name,
one with backwards "N's",
another with linking dashes
you call the letter train,
curly puffs of smoke
twirling around the
heart's edge.

We sit in the dining room,
oak table barely visible
beneath the scraps of
construction paper,
colored caps and pens,
full of valentines.

Your Daughter

To my mother

The ways I am like you
have shapes and sounds,
procedures and skills.

I see them in the mirror:
in the heart of hairline,
ladder narrow hips
and thin limbs.

I see it in my eyes
the way they flash and shine,
the sideways commas of expression
that frame them in a smile.

I hear it in my laugh,
as it pops out
in a jack-in-a-box burst,
the way it makes people
sitting in front of me
turn around.

I see it in the way I organize a meal,
everything arriving at the table
on time and warm,
glasses polished spot free.

I see it in the way I pay my bills:
always in full
on the date due,
no interest owed.

I feel it when I climb a trail,
each forward step unhindered
by miles or altitude,
determined I'll get to the top.

I feel it in the slivers of delight
that peek in like sun through blinds,
returning me for a moment
to the newness of a child's world—
these gifts of you
in me.

Lost

Holding the single blue mitten,
it struck me when she said,
"It's so small,"
as if I'd been forcing him
to wear something
long outgrown.

Why these tears?
We got our money's worth,
many season's of use.

Is it the size of
the one left,
showing how much
he's grown?

Or is it the window
I know I will stand at
after the door
has shut behind him,
in a future
made less distant
by a lost, blue mitten?

Haiku

Purple feather rose
the patter of your small feet
now gone forever

The Last Piano Recital

He discards the long-sleeved black shirt
for an over-sized Pink Floyd tee.
He is the only participant wearing sneakers,
like the white goose in the flock of Canadians
I saw filling the thawed portion of Grasmere Lake
this morning.
I tell myself it doesn't matter.

The girls glide to the bench
in long black skirts and
crisp, white blouses, their
thick, shiny hair
swept into ponytails.

My son is the thirteenth performer.
But I'm not superstitious.
The notes of Clementi's Sonatina in G Major
float through the air.
My husband and I grin.
This is music.
Can it be the same boy who hung an elaborate
sketch titled, "public urination" on the fridge?

Later at the reception, a group of little boys
playfully argue over who will get the first
piece of cake.
My son announces he will not be attending
the spring recital in May.

Perhaps I have heard for the last time
the tune of "O Susanna" banged out
by seven-year-olds.
Perhaps it is not surprising that
I dreamed of holding a small boy
in red corduroy overalls,
or that just today, I touched my
finger to the photo of those tiny feet
sprinkled with dirt.

One Thing

It came down to one thing:
I was afraid.
Terrified.
Everything around me was changing.
Parts of my dead neighbor's house
were being smashed by the new owner.
The backyard had turned into a grave
of torn down walls and nails.
I was leaving behind a
group of smart students
who loved me enough that
their sadness showed on
their blank faces.
My son was soon to be
off to college.
He was done with parental control.
Didn't want me making him food,
picking his dirty clothes
up off the floor, or
portioning out his monthly allowance
in $10-a-week chunks.
My whole world was upside down.
I felt old.

The bloom was off the flower of my life.
I was just waiting for the final shriveling.
Sometimes the return to earth
felt welcoming.
I'd had enough of trying to rise
to life's challenges.
But when you're a parent,
you can't give up.
I started to remember a teacher
who'd said I had a few novels in me.
I just hadn't taken the time
to write them.

Quiet Future

Your towel hangs
on the back of the door.
The soda sits
in the fridge.
Your room
still cluttered,
but empty of sound,
no thumping bass,
no voices of friends
coming through
the computer.

You left only one week ago,
but it hits me now
the way a bat hits
a spinning ball.

Even the cat seems to notice.
I blow my nose on the
rumpled dinner napkin
still on the table.
Take another bite of cantaloupe.
Push myself into
this quiet future,
without you in the house.

The Stars on the Ceiling

as the lights flick off
the stars on the ceiling
of your old room
begin to glow
an echo of your presence

now the room is dark

inside I run away
lose myself in a maze of canyons
following stream beds
drifting between the sandstone walls

searching for a new light
to replace what is gone

Epilogue

The saying is accurate: "Life goes on." Accordingly, the empty nest gave way to the formation of new dreams. A year after Canyon graduated from college, I decided to leave full-time teaching. A seminar I had attended at an earlier Yale reunion (my husband's alma mater) had impressed me with the notion that at sixty, one needs to step back and choose the direction of the next twenty years, rather than merely riding the same train without question.

Now I have an intriguing mix of activities, working as a relationship coach, a tutor, a creative writing instructor, and occasionally, substituting for former co-workers. The journey continues. It is a path of constant learning, of gratitude for the blessings I have and for the risks I've been willing to take.

Linda Keller
2015

Linda Keller

Author Linda Keller has been writing poetry since the age of thirteen. *Mother* is her 7th collection. Her previous books include: *Take It & Go On, Comet Dreams, Deep in the Wilderness, You Can Stop Longing* and the chapbooks, *Here I Am* and *Making Up the Way*. Her poems have appeared in a wide variety of anthologies and journals. Avid hikers, she and her husband divide their time between their homes in Denver and in the mountains near Leadville, Colorado.

My blog is *www.ljkeller.com*

From a drawing with Tigger, Pooh, Piglet and Eeyore by Canyon, when he was six

Dedication

This collection is dedicated to my son, H. Canyon Boak, who started as an idea in my head, and then filled my dreams. He helped me overcome my fears as I reached into the fullness of life and its unpredictability. Thank you for teaching me the depth of love and for becoming even more than what I imagined possible.

Recommendations

"Linda Keller's deliciously vivid poems highlight the kinds of motherhood moments from pregnancy to empty nest that make mothering so potent and meaningful. A great gift for any young mom to help her to cherish her own motherhood moments...and for grandmothers as well as to augment their grandmomming."

— Susan Heitler, Ph.D., author of *The Power of Two, a guide to marriage success.*

"The earnest, beautiful snapshots of the ages and stages of a child's genesis and growth from the perspective of a mother's heart, arms and mind are priceless."

— Annette Tilleman-Dick, mother of eleven